Biff's Wonder Words

Written by Kate Ruttle and Annemarie Young,
based on original characters created by
Roderick Hunt and Alex Brychta
Illustrated by Alex Brychta

OXFORD

UNIVERSITY PRESS

Help me read these words.
Can you find them in the picture?

Mum
Dad

dog, duck, door, drum, duckling, dandelion

5

Read these words and
find them in the picture.

dog

cat

log, frog, bog

7

Read these words and
find them in the picture.

mud

cap

web

water, wind, woodpecker

Read these words and find them in the picture.

bag

hat

pen

nut, mat, cat

Can you find two other things in the picture that end with **t**?

Read these words and find them in the picture. Which words rhyme?

man

bus

cab

van

can, pan

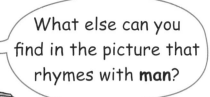

What else can you find in the picture that rhymes with **man**?

Read these words and
find them in the picture.

sun

cup

jam

log

Chip, cup, sheep

15

Read these words and find them in the picture. Which words rhyme?

hen

bug

leg

den

den, pen

17

Read these words and
find them in the picture.

mop

pot

mug

lid

tap

pot, dot, fruit, bucket, biscuit

How many things can you find that end in **t**?

19

Read these words and
find them in the picture.

Biff

rug

bed

mess

sock

clock, mug, head

21

Spot the difference

Find the five differences in the two pictures of Biff.